Ignite
INSPIRATION

MOTIVATING ENTREPRENEURS TO ACHIEVE WORK LIFE BALANCE AND STAY ON TOP OF BUSINESS TRENDS TO EASILY SCALE BUSINESS

Lucy Hoger

Published by Lucy Hoger

Copyright © by Lucy Hoger

All rights reserved. This book, or parts thereof, may not be reproduced in any form without permission.

First edition April 2016

Motivation is the cornerstone of all achievement in our personal lives as well as in our business lives. Without motivation, nothing worthwhile happens. For Daily Motivation and Advice that will move you to succeed beyond any challenge and inspire you to never give up, visit: Visionocity_Magazine on Instagram.

Contents

DEDICATION 5

7 TRENDS TO INSPIRE OTHERS 7

ATTITUDE 31

CHARACTER 49

CONFIDENCE 71

FOCUS 89

INSPIRATION 105

STRENGTH 121

ONE FINAL THOUGHT 135

ABOUT THE AUTHOR 137

DEDICATION

This book is dedicated to the man who has shown me:

Life is an adventure;

Learning is a lifelong passion;

Curiosity opens new worlds;

Persistence creates a winner;

Laughter lightens any burden;

Love-at-first-sight is possible and eternal.

To my best friend and husband,

Anthony "Sonny" Hoger

7 TRENDS TO INSPIRE OTHERS

Motivation is the cornerstone of all achievement, whether in our personal lives or in business. Without motivation, nothing worthwhile happens. Although the study of what motivates people has been around for a long time, it is the methods of delivering that motivation which have evolved exponentially over the last 30 years or so. Most recently, the way people seek and absorb their prescription of daily inspiration has changed dramatically. This has been mainly caused by modern technology and its offspring: Social Media. Demands on our personal time have vastly increased, creating a need for constant dosages of motivation to keep us focused and working on our bigger goals. In business, for instance, motivation has been transformed and enhanced by adding more meaningful value qualities for our employees, our customers, partners and anyone else connected to our business. Motivation today has many facets that determine its ultimate effectiveness: positive encouragement, monetary and mental incentive, use of subtle persuasion, emotional and sensory stimulus, appeal to personal drive, and other catalyst-driven components that can create outstanding results.

To better understand how the delivery of motivation has evolved, I have studied seven evolutional trends of traditional motivational methodology taught by industry leaders such as Tony Robbins, Daniel Pink, Stephen Covey, and Simon Sinek. One of the main sources of my research began by following the mentorship of Nathan Chan, CEO of *Foundr Magazine*. In three years, Nathan has created a content media empire from his top-ranked 10 'Business and Investing' magazine on the Apple Newsstand, highly listened to Podcats and blogs. He has interviewed such business giants as Sir Richard Branson, Tony Robbins, Guy Kawasaki, Tim Ferris and Gary Vaynerchuck. His goal is to support entrepreneurs worldwide with business insights that are working in today's fast-paced environment. He continues to share his insight through his educational programs. Nathan's Instagram account, Foundr_Magazine, has gained in excess of 700,000 followers in about a year and a half. Nathan has been my mentor in growing my own Instagram account, Visionocity_Magazine to over 200,000 in about one-and-a-half year.

The emerging trends outlined in this book are based on my interactions with my followers as well has having built a network of influence on Social Media. Additional awareness was developed from my own Apple Newsstand publication of my digital magazine, and frequent collaboration with many entrepreneurs and other business owners I have met throughout my 40-year corporate career. I have summarized the results of these evolutional trends below.

Motivational Evolution #1: Long-term Blueprint versus Practical Next Steps

In Stephen Covey's national best-selling book, *The 7 Habits of Highly Effective People*, he writes about the need to put "first things first." Meaning, we have several roles that we play in our lives, which must be balanced throughout the day. He was an early adopter and advocate of the Work/Life balance concept. Covey described how to manage the various moving pieces in our lives to create this perfect balance. He explained how we play several roles throughout our lives. His advice includes creating a blueprint of what you must do to fulfill each and every role by planning your week with a set of accomplishments you must achieve. Examples of these roles include categories such as: Individual, Wife/Husband, Mother/Father, Real Estate Salesperson, Sunday School Teacher, Manager and Symphony Board Member. The list can be extensive and overwhelming, not to mention the time it takes planning exactly what needs to be done to perform each role each week. This blueprint approach to our daily lives was introduced fifteen years ago with the publication of Covey's book, and our society has been dramatically changed for the better by his guidance. But times change and society has become more complex. Though it is important to know the overall blueprint his charts and teachings provide, given our fast-paced lifestyle people are also looking for practical and immediate useful next steps to find guidance. They have an immediate problem to solve and need some quick relief for their dilemma. It is in our nature to seek fast solutions. We have become impatient with long processes and often want a speedy answer to a difficult problem.

This evolution occurred as we began seeing increasing demands on our time. We no longer have complete control over our personal time with the introduction of numerous faster technologies and new ways of communication such as emails, texts, tweets, instant messages, chats, photos, and videos. Social media began dominating our everyday world from the important news of the day to family updates, sprinkled with the silly, must-see cat videos that have gone viral and everyone is talking about.

7 TRENDS TO INSPIRE OTHERS

The instantaneous communication and access to information have exponentially expanded the volume of data we must process every day. When Steven Covey wrote his book, we had three common ways of communicating: phone call, email or fax. Today, when someone needs to ask a question, they no longer pick-up the phone and call us; they send us a text and expect a reply within minutes. We have changed the way we communicate with one another and, in most cases, removed the polite pleasantries of a salutation; we get straight to the point. Social media platforms like Facebook and YouTube become almost addictive as they learn what we like to see and constantly present streams of new content that make it hard to step away from our mobile device and look up at the world around us.

The influence of today's technology and our patterns of communication have changed the way we receive and process our information. We think in quick sound-bites, removing anything we think is unnecessary. We no longer take the time to do extensive critical thinking about the various roles we play in our lives and how we use these roles to manage our lives. Rather, we want quick answers, "a silver-bullet" solution if you will. If we have a specific pressing problem, we are looking for a practical and specific solution ... NOW!

Motivational Evolution #2: General Self-help versus Personalized Expert Advice

Tony Robbins exploded onto the motivational stage through his infomercial and accompanying national best-selling book, *Awaken The Giant Within*. In his seminars and book, Tony discussed, in detail, each aspect of self-empowerment along with countless stories and quotes that reinforced his lessons. To assist his readers in their self-improvement journey, Tony created a plan called "The Seven Days to Shape Your Life."

Through his books and seminars, Tony encourages us to create our own transformation by equipping us with toolkits, with resources and methods that have been used by his numerous followers to bring about their long-term change. In contrast, today, people are looking for personalized expert advice that is driven by instant gratification. Experts no longer have to be best-selling book authors to deliver their message thanks to the development and growth of Social Media.

YouTube is one of those preeminent sources used to dispense this type of advice and encouragement filled with personal stories of their life's journeys from struggle to success. People are looking for real-time advice that meets their personal specific challenge.

This shift highlights the need to analyze and understand the audience's expectations from the delivered message and advice rather than just blanketing a generic message across the Social Media landscape.

In the past, national motivation speakers have taken their adversity and experiences and used their situations to motivate and inspire themselves to create a successful life. For example, Tony Robbins talks about his early days when he lived in a small apartment, washing his dishes in the bathtub, and was morbidly overweight. He was miserable until he decided to change his life and start his journey to becoming successful. Today, Tony outlines and teaches the steps he took to create, achieve and maintain his success. People attend his seminars by the thousands, but recently a new set of motivational speakers has emerged on the scene.

Seminar attendees want assurances that the speaker/motivator has experienced the same **exact** problem they are trying to solve. For example, Marie Osmond openly shares that she was 50 pounds overweight and now uses a nationally recognized weight-loss program and meal replacement regimen to keep "show biz" beautiful. Other celebrities are featured on TV ads promoting other weight-loss programs. The point is these celebrities are addressing a specific problem with the message, "If I can do this, you can do this." Also, the key is that they are not talking about multiple problems like health issues, combined with drug problems and a weight problem, and so on. They are addressing one problem at a time. They tell about being overwhelmed and how they overcame their challenges to obtain their success. The audience feels empathy that they have "walked a mile in my shoes" and the expert directly relates to their specific problem through direct experience. The operative word is *direct*. As long as the message and experience relate to the audience, the expert's advice is believable, personal and accepted.

In the past, the expert/speaker would address everyone in the audience with the intention of serving them all equally. In reality though, only specific members of the audience could relate to what was being said by piecing together the message the expert was offering. Then it was up to those listening to create their own plan of action. Today, people are seeking highly targeted, personalized advice that can articulate exactly how they are feeling, what they are thinking, and how they see themselves. Today's experts must appeal to the audience, in their exact life experience, before the audience will buy the product being offered or take advice and mentorship. Because of this experience, almost anyone can become an "overnight sensation" if they can solve a problem that thousands are clamoring to immediately solve because it's causing them pain right now.

Motivational Evolution #3: Individually-Focused Purpose versus Community-Driven Purpose

Daniel Pink's *New York Times* best-selling book, *Drive: The Surprising Truth About What Motivates Us*, emphasizes that we are motivated by our autonomy, mastery and purpose. He proves that money in and of itself is not the sole motivator instrumental in creating change. At the core of motivation is seeking purpose and meaning in life. We are often told that once we have learned our purpose in life we will be happier to pursue our dream. We read books and go to seminars, but the reality is that few of us can ever effectively articulate our ultimate purpose. Purpose has rapidly morphed from a personal mission into becoming part of a community and becoming an advocate for a cause. This is not limited to the "Millennials"; it applies to every generation.

Tony Robbins teaches that one of the six basic human fulfillment needs is that "we seek to contribute beyond ourselves." This may be the reason why cause-based communities have become an everyday occurrence. If you are operating a business, creating a community of client advocates will strengthen the all-important foundation of your business. On a purely personal front, we happily increase our sense of fulfillment.

A shift has taken place from the individual-focused purpose to a community-driven purpose. In the past, we were taught that we could get anything we wanted by using intimidation tactics.

And we were encouraged to do this in Robert Ringer's best-selling book, *Winning Through Intimidation*, published in 1975. In the 1987 film *Wall Street*, the main character, Gordon Gekko (portrayed by Michael Douglas), proclaimed "greed is good." It became a mantra for some. We can find scores of movies and books that all promote the same thing: survival of the fittest. It's an attitude that promotes win-lose scenarios. That is, in order to win, someone else must lose. Life is a zero-sum game.

Today, we have moved from the "me" mentality to the "we" mentality. If you ask someone to describe their life's purpose, only a small minority of the population would be able to do that. You'd get mainly blank stares resembling a "deer in the headlights" look. When we change the discussion to their causes, crusades and/or grand-mission, people will immediately list a handful of organizations and companies they support through their time, money and other resources.

Companies have created a loyal following by adopting a community of advocate customers for a specific cause. Take Toms Shoes, for example. For every pair of shoes that the customers purchase, a portion of the sale goes to help a person in need. They call their campaign "One for One". They believe, "Through your purchase, TOMS helps provide shoes, sight, water, safe birth and bullying prevention services to people in need." Now we have a choice when we buy a pair of shoes: to make a fashion statement by buying a pair of Manolos or to contribute to a needy child by buying a pair of Toms shoes.

This shift has transcended generations. No longer is it just the Millennials who are championing this community-driven and purpose-focused advocacy; they have led the way to every generation seeking to belong to a community. With Social Media, instantaneous news, and ever donating to a tragic occurrence through

Crowdfunding websites, anyone, from anywhere, at any time can become an advocate for any cause and feel like that makes a difference today.

Motivational Evolution #4: Weekend Intensive Training versus Bite-Size/On-Demand Delivery

T. Harv Ecker revolutionized training for his huge audiences ten years ago using *his New York Times, Wall Street Journal*, and *USA Today* bestseller, *Secrets of the Millionaire Mind: Mastering the Inner Game of Wealth*. Enclosed with each book sold, Harv included two free tickets to the Millionaire Mind Intensive Seminar. It was conducted over an extensive, content-packed, threeday weekend event allowing the reader to delve deeper into the principles discussed in his book.

Many industry leaders still conduct weekend intensive motivational training sessions. After such a three-day seminar, the participant leaves in a state of euphoria, feeling that they can conquer the world. That is a good thing.

A month after the event though, the once highly-motivated participant falls back into many of the same old thought patterns as before. While some people will continue to attend these types of events in the hope of finding that special spark for change again, the current economic environment has changed how people prefer to consume this type of lengthy motivational endurance event, namely a shorter time commitment.

Moreover, our modern attention span has significantly shrunk. Studies have shown our average attention span has decreased from 12 seconds in 2000 to only 8.25 seconds in 2015, according to information published by Statistic Brain[1]. Would you believe the study revealed that a goldfish has an attention span of 9 seconds?

What does this all boil down to?

In my experience, four training delivery criteria have emerged: (1) remote training availability to be consumed at any time, (2) the advice provided must be in bite-size amounts, easy to digest with immediate actionable recommendations, (3) content must be made available in different learning modalities, for example, video, audio, downloadable worksheets, etc., and (4) access to the expert is mandatory throughout the learning experience. Experts who are able to deliver training under these conditions can create a lasting, loyal community.

Furthermore, people want the option to have the expert work alongside them in a do-it-withyou model.

And, for those who are seeking immediate results, if possible, they want the experts to do-it-for-them.

In the past, executive and business seminar gurus would create a weekend intensive event where thousands of people would come hear them talk about their experience. It usually took place during a Friday, Saturday and Sunday timeframe. After they gave their lecture, they would invite you to continue learning their lessons from the audio/video recordings and books they had for sale in the back of the room and lobby. The members in the audience would furiously take notes on what they heard. But, alas, for the most part, Monday morning started with their usual same-old routine and by Friday many of the great new ideas they'd scribbled in their notebooks were forgotten and never to be acted upon, either now or in the future.

Taking advantage of the wisdom taught during the entire weekend experience would not be realized for most in the audience.

This scenario continues today with experts from the online marketing community to practitioners in health care conferences. But desires are changing. Audiences are seeking a different type of training. They want education-on-demand as a service to solve their problem, similar to the style of many on-line universities with their web-based lectures.

As I discussed earlier, we have a time shortage problem and are seeking the most direct path to answering our questions as soon as possible. People are willing to pay for this quick access to this expertise. They are seeking wisdom that can be applied immediately rather than just information that needs to be sorted out before any action can occur. People are looking for bite-size, on-demand delivery of information that can be consumed within 20 minutes.

They want the information to get straight to the point and be supported with the necessary reference documents that will quicken their learning. They also want a community they can interact and communicate with (often created on Facebook) to exchange ideas, ask questions and find experts within the community. In some cases, the on-line community will take on a life of its own.

Training has become a 360 degree experience, rather than one-way communication, similar to the traditional teacher/student relationship.

Motivational Evolution #5: Advice Handbooks versus LifeHacks (Short Cuts)

Prolific writer John Maxwell has written more than 75 books and is recognized as an authority on business leadership. He has trained leaders from nearly every country in the world, including presidents of nations and Fortune 500 companies. He teaches us that leadership is about motivating and influencing your organization to act in concert toward a common goal. And he has taught a number of well-trained experts that can help any business create this transformation through detailed seminars.

There will always be people who want to fully understand this subject and are excited to see this volume of work offered. Yet, recent growing trends find ready-made shortcuts to quickly answer a specific question or circumstance. This trend is called "LifeHacks". You can find a "Hack" for productivity, success, motivation, communications, etc.

People want to model billionaires and millionaires, and want quick references to their business philosophy, everyday routines, books they read, their mindset, and their views on life. The list can be extensive, but can be found with a simple search on the internet where a number of blogs, websites, and Social Media posts will offer the sought-after insights within a few minutes by sorting through the myriad of sources available.

The best-selling authors, specializing in the business and motivational arenas, have written a series of books that can be viewed as advice handbooks. They are filled with valuable insights on a variety of ideas and strategies and are often embellished with personal stories of struggles and victories. Beyond the personal touch, they highlight how other great leaders were able to overcome the odds and achieve their success. But many of the books are over 250 pages in length and can be time-consuming for people to read cover-to-cover and retain the information easily, as a shorter booklet would allow you to do.

Over the past decade, blog articles have become more popular than lengthy books because they provide concise insights that the reader is seeking. This is an alternative to reading an entire book, to extract the immediately useful information that is needed to solve a specific problem. In today's lexicon, these shortcuts are termed LifeHacks.

With the introduction of Social Media, people often seek LifeHacks from sources other than books and blogs. Most Millennials would rather get advice from YouTube and watch a short how-to video on solving a problem. If you learn best through auditory methods, then Podcast is the most trusted source, especially for those who like to multi-task. They find a series of podcasts and download them into their cell phone and mobile device and off they go performing their daily activity like running, jogging, and doing errands. For the more visual learner, Pinterest is the perfect source for Do-It-Yourself (DIY) projects.

Not only are LifeHacks readily available, they can be accessed in a variety of learning methods. People are no longer interested in the detailed background of a topic, they want to get in and get out as quickly as possible. It all goes back to the limited amount of time we all have in getting everything done in a day. No one gets more than 24 hours.

Motivational Evolution #6: Emphasis on the Overall Potential versus Short-term Results

Rhonda Byrne became a best-selling author nearly ten years ago with her blockbuster book, *The Secret*. It is based on using the Law of Attraction and the power of positive thinking to create life-changing events. Her book sold more than 19 million copies worldwide and has been translated into 46 languages[2]. The book was a commercial success and the experts that appear on its accompanying DVD, also called *The Secret*, benefited from the phenomena.

The challenge is that the power of positive thinking, *wishing and hoping* for overall success in every area of our lives, usually does not create lasting results without a lot of positively hard work to achieve our desired outcome. People are savvier today than they were ten years ago. Now they will thoroughly research a product or service before considering making their final purchase. This behavior spills over into choosing their sources of motivation. People seek more than just a momentary emotional boost of confidence that does not last long. They are looking for tangible results to prove that the advice worked. They want testimonials supporting the real changes that others have experienced. These testimonials are paramount to the motivational advice seeker. They want to know that it works before they invest their precious time and money into a program.

As highlighted in *The Secret*, The Law of Attraction, vision boards, and positive thinking will only get someone so far. Yes, they can help change someone's attitude toward a negative experience or help them rise above their current improvised situation and circumstances, and they can create an extraordinary mental picture of the life they wish to live. But self-limiting beliefs have held them back for as long as they have because no one has taken the time to teach them a better way. Once their limiting beliefs are changed and new possibilities allowed to emerge, a new chapter in their lives can begin.

It begs this question: Now what? They must see the potential that the future holds for them. They have a high-level idea of what they want to do, who they want to be and what they want

to have. So the next step is to create a plan to take action. The most critical step that needs to be taken is to create an action plan that creates momentum toward a stated goal, otherwise known as "imperfect action", and trying something new.

Discouragement may set in if readers try and try and try again with no results. That's why the changing of their belief systems must be complemented with a plan that will get them shortterm positive results. For example, Nutrisystem, a leading weight-loss program, promotes losing 5 pounds in the first week as a form of "quick start, quick results" for the customer to experience.

Plus, they have a 30-day money back guarantee if the customer is not satisfied. Cosmetic companies promise their customers that their wrinkles can disappear in days by using their facial products. The idea is: quick results, satisfied customer.

With the national brands constantly promising overnight results, it is little wonder that the promise of an overall potential only goes so far. To motivate people into action, we need to make a promise of immediate results even if it is simply the first step of a much longer process.

Motivational Evolution #7: Soft and Supportive Language versus Bold and Direct Communications

Oprah Winfrey created her own brand of interviewing style by using soft and supportive questioning while still asking poignant and probing questions. She makes the interviewee comfortable discussing their story. There is a high-level of politeness about her while she seeks the truth from her guests. Many have modeled her style of communication over the years to create their own brand and style.

Our language pattern, however, has dramatically changed over the past few years to one that is bolder and more direct. People want to be directed in what to think about a situation, rather than being guided through a process that helps develop their own conclusion. That is why the diet book series *Eat This Not That* became so popular. It is direct and simple.

I have noticed that attention grabbing headlines are becoming more provocative. While the supportive communication style is still a welcomed form of motivation, long motivational stories and descriptions have given way to shorter, more concise, direct, and bold ones.

In the past, communications were written and sent through emails with obligatory salutations and normal pleasantries of a letter at the beginning of the email. This was followed by long explanations and backstories before getting to the actionable request or point. Emails were filled with language and common courtesy.

While this style and means of communication is still part of our routine lives, new forms of communication have emerged with the introduction of Social Media. Emails have given way to 144 Twitter characters or less. To cram our message into 144 characters, acronyms and abbreviations were introduced to express, in as few characters as possible, what would have taken a few sentences to describe. For example, OMG, LOL, BRB, :), are quick to type into a text and still get the message across. This creates a specialized language among Millennials to describe their thoughts and emotions. Finally, Emoji (smiley faces, etc.) were introduced to help us express our emotion in a single character. Not to mention, four letter words and profanity are now commonplace in our daily written communications.

This new style of writing messages has created a blunt, direct method of expressing one's thoughts, ideas, concepts, and questions. Cursive writing is no longer taught in some schools since learning is done on tablets and computers. The reality is that our current generation may not be able to read The Declaration of Independence or Constitution, much less comprehend their meaning because of the changes in how we convey our thoughts today.

Though soft and supportive language still has a place in our society, in many cases, a bold and direct communication is replacing this practice in some segments of our society.

Final Word...

Inspiration and motivational concepts are changing with the times as they apply to both our personal and professional lives. While the traditional methods work and often are still widely sought after, the seven emerging trends just mentioned compliment and sometimes replace other forms of persuasion and encouragement styles in use today.

The remainder of this book represents 90 motivational posts that resulted in the most popular number of engagements from my Visionocity Magazine Instagram account. Every post is accompanied by my perspective on the famous quote and a take-action item designed to reinforce the motivational message.

I hope you enjoy them and learn from them as I did.

> Staying ahead of business trends is only one part of creating a prosperous business. To receive a proven formula that can help any business become and remain successful, download your free report, www.wiredforresults.com, revealing a seven step formula based on time-tested principles that will create a positive impact on your bottom line.

---

(1) http://www.statisticbrain.com/attention-span-statistics/
(2) https://en.wikipedia.org/wiki/The_Secret_%28book%29
(3) "The Hindustan Times". The Hindustan Times. 2010-07-16. Retrieved 2013-07-29.

ATTITUDE

ATTITUDE

1

Big results require big ambitions. — **Heraclitus**

Without ambition, we will remain frozen in the same place year after year. Ambition is the key to any success, just ask any person who has amassed great wealth. It is what separates the dreamers from the champions. But ambition alone will not singularly drive ultimate success. The ability to collaborate with others is equally as important as having big ambitions. By combining the skills and talents of others, larger results will emerge rather than trying to create your desired outcome alone.

TAKE ACTION: Create a team aligned with your same goals and ambitions and then create results that will last a lifetime.

ATTITUDE

2

Clear your mind of can't. — **Samuel Johnson**

One of the biggest obstacles to success is the word "can't". It limits our thinking as to what is possible in life. Just because it has never been done before does not mean we are not meant to be the first ones that can do it and succeed. When we remove limiting words like "can't", new ways of thinking and possibilities begin to open up for us. We have unlimited potential locked up inside us. Do not let "can't" instill the fear that stops you. TAKE ACTION: Have confidence that you are on the right path and that you will succeed and achieve your dream.

ATTITUDE

3

Your time is limited so don't waste it living someone else's life. **—Steve Jobs**

We are born to be unique and stand above the crowd. Like Steve Jobs, we need to embrace who we are no matter what others think or say about us and our ideas. People who have inspired the world were driven by their vision to create a better tomorrow for others. They lived their own lives and followed their own passions even though others may have disapproved and called them crazy. TAKE ACTION: Follow your passions and dreams without worrying about what others think.

ATTITUDE

4

Forget all the reasons why something doesn't work. You only need to find one good reason why it will.
— **Robert Anthony**

We give ourselves many reasons why we should not act on a new opportunity. These reasons will have us fail before we even start. That's just the fear inside us trying to protect us from getting hurt. We simply need one good reason that will inspire us to try something new. This reason will become our life's mission that creates something much bigger than us. That one decision can create an incredible success. TAKE ACTION: Decide to take a risk and try something new today.

ATTITUDE

5

*It doesn't matter where you come from.
All that matters is where you're going.*
— **Bob Marley**

Successful people come from different backgrounds and different circumstances. It is the determination, drive, and tenacity that produces extraordinary results over time. Where we started is of little importance. It is the obstacles that stand in our way that will ultimately make us stronger. These obstacles will shape our story and inspire others to break through their own challenges. We never know whose role model we may become. We are the only ones who can define our future. TAKE ACTION: Focus on where you are going, not where you have been.

ATTITUDE

6

Nothing can stop the man with the right mental attitude from achieving his goal. Nothing on earth can help the man with the wrong mental attitude.
— **Thomas Jefferson**

Attitude plays a tremendous part in attaining any goal. Henry Ford's saying is as true today as it was when he originally said it, "Whether you think you can, or you think you can't — you're right." Entrepreneurs are people who think anything is possible. It is the individual's mental readiness that envisions in the mind and heart what can be created in the real world. Leaders throughout history have shown that the right mental attitude can make the impossible possible. TAKE ACTION: Change your attitude, be positive, drive toward your goals, and anything is possible.

ATTITUDE

7

People may hear your words, but they feel your attitude. — **John Maxwell**

What we say to get our message across is one thing. How we say it, our attitude, will show the commitment and conviction we have to carry out our message. When people see, in our eyes and body language, how much we want our dreams and goals, they will not question "if" we are going to make it; they will be talking about "when" we are going to make it. We know that our attitude toward any situation will change the outcome and position us for success. TAKE ACTION: Create an attitude of expectancy toward your dreams and goals, and attract what you want and deserve.

ATTITUDE

8

People rarely succeed unless they have fun in what they are doing. — **Dale Carnegie**

Success is more than working hard every day; it is loving what we do. We have to have fun and enjoy the journey along the way. Without fun, the daily routine can get to be too much and cause us to quit on our dream too soon. Successful people cannot tell the difference between work and play because they love what they do every day. They do not have the concept of taking a vacation because they are `committed' to their dream. TAKE ACTION: Go have some fun and build it big. Take a break for a few days and get a new perspective on your dream if you are not having fun or loving what you do.

ATTITUDE

9

The best way to guarantee a loss is to quit.
— **Morgan Freeman**

We know that the only way we will *never* be successful is if we quit altogether. Many people quit before they even begin. Challenges, setbacks, and failures are part of the journey toward success. Morgan Freeman knows firsthand that sticking with his vision of success helped him become one of the most recognized actors in Hollywood. We need to follow his example and never give up no matter how difficult things become. TAKE ACTION: Become determined that any circumstances and setbacks only create learning experiences, but, no matter what, never quit.

ATTITUDE

10

The greatest barrier to success is the fear of failure.
— **S.G. Ericsson**

We were born to win, but sometimes our fears will hold us back. Most commonly, it is the fear of the unknown that causes us to stop and think twice about taking a risk by doing something new. We must not let fear paralyze us into non-action. Risk, and its accompanying feeling of fear, is part of the journey, and we must push past this artificial barrier. Success is waiting for us. What we have to do is get past that doorway labeled fear to claim our prize. TAKE ACTION: Face your greatest fears, stare them straight in the eye, and act in spite of them.

ATTITUDE

11

The only failure is not to try. — **George Clooney**

There is no reward without risk. There is no victory without failure. There is no comeback without a setback. Some people create dream lists and vision boards but never take action. They are afraid of failure. That is not how we think. We know that failure is just part of the price that must be paid to create our ultimate results. We are crazy enough to try anything that gets us closer to success because we are not afraid of failure. Failure teaches us valuable lessons that show us the way to our ultimate victory. TAKE ACTION: Accept failure as part of our learning process, knowing it is just a step on our journey to reach our ultimate goal.

ATTITUDE

12

The voice in your head that says "you can't do this" is a liar. —Robert H. Schuller

When we doubt ourselves, we limit our possibilities and the opportunities that we dream of having one day. Success Rule #1 is to believe in ourselves so others can believe in our vision and join us on our quest. We all have that little voice inside our heads telling us we cannot accomplish our dreams. We need to find the strength to ignore those negative thoughts and say, "What the mind can conceive we can achieve." We are masters of our own destiny as long as we believe. TAKE ACTION: Increase your belief that you *can*, and you *will* achieve each and every goal you have set for yourself.

ATTITUDE

13

Whenever I hear "It can't be done," I know I'm close to success. — **Michael Flatley**

We are inspired by a good challenge, especially when people tell us, "It can't be done." If they would spend as much time figuring out how it can be done, imagine how many more great success stories we could recount. Instead, it is easier for people to live in their world of negativity. We are constantly looking for ways to create something better for ourselves and the world around us. That is the only path we know to our success because we are the champions of our own triumph. TAKE ACTION: Ignore the negative talk from others and focus on what can be done to get you closer to your goal. Ignore the naysayers.

ATTITUDE

14

You cannot change the circumstances, but you can change yourself. — **Jim Rohn**

Having a positive outlook regardless of the circumstances will change any situation. This is how we move beyond any obstacles. We cannot control how people think and act, but we can change how we react to their drama. By not getting caught in the noise from the crowd, we will rise above it to follow our dream and succeed. Many great leaders, inventors, and titans of industry have risen above their circumstances to achieve greatness. This includes Abraham Lincoln, who never won one election until he was elected President of the United States. TAKE ACTION: Change how you see yourself and the world regardless of your obstacles.

ATTITUDE

15

You miss 100% of the shots you don't take.
— **Wayne Gretzky**

We have to be willing to take risks in order to get what we want. Playing it safe may guarantee a stable lifestyle, but we will never get ahead and create our dreams by being meek. If we play it 'safe', we are going backward because life moves forward, actually away from us, at a fast pace. Daring to dream means that we dare and take risks and set trends for others to follow. Wayne Gretzky was nicknamed "The Great One" and is called "the greatest hockey player ever" by acclaimed sportswriters. He took every shot he could and has scored over 200 points in one season. TAKE ACTION: Take as many shots as you can at your dream. For every 9 rejections, there will be someone who eventually says, "Yes."

ATTITUDE

For continued motivation that will encourage you to develop an attitude of perseverance toward achieving your goals, visit **Visionocity_Magazine** on Instagram.

CHARACTER

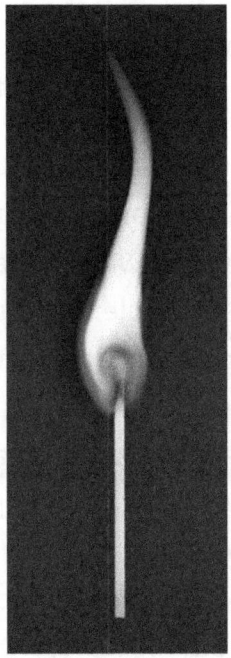

CHARACTER

1

Show class, have pride and display character. If you do, winning takes care of itself.— **Paul Bryant**

We know that one way to reach for success is through hard work. It is our work ethic and determination that will set the example for others that success is possible. Others will see the pride in our work and that will attract the right opportunities and people into our lives. The daily habit we create will set us apart from others who are simply working on their goals part time. By focusing on what we can control and our actions, winning becomes the result of simple efforts we do every day. TAKE ACTION: Take pride in everything you do and become a person of character. Winning will find the moment to take care of itself.

CHARACTER

2

Circumstances do not make a man. They reveal him.
— **James Allen**

Circumstances reveal the character of who we really are and who we are becoming. As we move through our circumstances, we are known for our generosity and willingness to help others regardless of our situation. That is who we are and why we stand out in people's minds. It is during the difficult times that we learn, deep at our core, who we are and we will be surprised at what we find. It is that strong character that suddenly reveals itself that may have been hidden for quite some time. TAKE ACTION: Push past your greatest fear to reveal the inner character of who you are.

CHARACTER

3

Don't let other people tell you what you want.
— **Pat Railey**

We do not need to listen to other people's opinions about what we should do, what we should think, and what we should be. If we try to please everyone, we will become average just like them. Coach Pat Riley won 2012 and 2013 NBA Championships for the Miami Heat and has been named Coach of the Year three times. He has coached some of the best talent in basketball. Neither he nor any of his players have ever changed who they are to please their critics. That is why they are champions. TAKE ACTION: Stand for what you want without concern for what others think.

CHARACTER

4

Don't let someone else's opinion of you become your reality. **—Les Brown**

We often think about how other people see us. Do they like us? What do they think of us? If we start to change ourselves into what other people think we should be, we will lose our sense of who we really are. We must stay true to who we are and must not let other people's opinions change what we are. We have many important things to create in this world. Remember, opinions do not pay bills, put food on the table or create a future. We are a work-in-process, and we must remain excited about what we are becoming. TAKE ACTION: Be gentle with yourself when dealing with other people's opinions. Do not pay for their opinion with the rest of your life.

CHARACTER

5

**Dream as if you'll live forever, live as if you'll die today.
— LeBron James**

Champions know what it takes to turn their dreams into reality. They know the meaning of hard work. More importantly, they give their every effort, every day, to become champions for the rest of their lives. They know how to dream BIG dreams. They know it is how you play the game that is played each day that counts. Hard work, determination, persistence, and tenacity are but a few of the words used to describe these champions. They set an example for the rest of us. That is the roadmap to success. Maybe it is not the exact steps or formula we need, but the path is clear. TAKE ACTION: Dream big. Live today fully and completely. No regrets.

CHARACTER

6

Honesty is a very expensive gift. Don't expect it from cheap people. — **Warren Buffet**

In life, as in business, we expect people to be honest and have integrity. We expect them to keep their word whenever they make a promise. However, even Warren Buffet has experienced people who are less than honest when he is making deals for his business. Warren calls these people "cheap" not because they are tightwads, but because they are poor in character. As he says, our honesty is the most expensive gift we can give someone. TAKE ACTION: Be a person of character and integrity in every part of your life. But remember, others must earn your trust.

CHARACTER

7

*If you really want to do something, you'll find a way.
If you don't, you'll find an excuse.*
— Dwayne "The Rock" Johnson

"Where there's a will, there's a way," so goes the saying. When we want something bad enough, we will move Heaven and Earth to make it happen. We are so focused on our dream that we can feel it in our hands. Yet others will find excuses why they are not working toward their dreams, blaming it on an array of "circumstances", which are reasons for their lack of action. We recognize those reasons as excuses, and we waste no time on them. TAKE ACTION: Find a way, never settle for an excuse. Focus and pursue your dream.

CHARACTER

8

If you're lucky enough to be different, don't ever change. **—Taylor Swift**

Taylor Swift's quote has meaning for those of us who think and act differently than the crowd. We do things our way. Yet, we are able to get results that make a difference in other people's lives. Being different can be just the right spark needed to take our idea to the next level. What makes us stand out from the masses is that we are willing to work hard every day and create our own success. That part of us will never change because we are the champions of our dreams for a better tomorrow. TAKE ACTION: Embrace who you are and make a difference in the lives of others.

CHARACTER

9

Everything negative - pressure, challenges - is an opportunity for me to rise. —**Kobe Bryant**

Champions are always under pressure to perform at their highest level. They see these pressures and challenges as opportunities to rise to the occasion and win. Each of us is a champion in our own way. We face our own pressures and challenges. But we have a choice in how we will deal with them. We are success-driven and will overcome any obstacle that comes our way. We are champions in our own game as long as we keep forging ahead every day toward our goals. TAKE ACTION: Turn every negative thought into an opportunity and rise to greatness.

CHARACTER

10

It's hard to beat a person who never gives up.
— **Babe Ruth**

When people see the determination in your eyes, they know that you will accomplish what you have set out to do. There is no turning back or giving up. Just press forward. People are admired for their tenacity when they overcome their obstacles and achieve their goals. There are many ways to get there: through the wall, around the wall, or over the wall. The point is we must continue to try new ways of winning until we succeed. This is what sets us apart from the crowd. TAKE ACTION: Keep a strong, positive attitude about winning and never give up.

CHARACTER

11

Losers make promises they often break. Winners make commitment they always keep. — **Denis Waitley**

As winners, we keep our word and our commitment to act and deliver on our promise. Relationships are built on the trust that everyone will act in the best interest of the others. We have had experiences where people have not kept their word. Some of them may have had a good reason beyond their control but when it comes to those who continually promise and never deliver or under deliver, it is time to move on and work with someone who will support our efforts. "How we do anything is how we do everything" is a motto to keep in mind from T. Harv Ecker. We are winners because we keep our commitments. TAKE ACTION: Build relationships that last based on integrity.

CHARACTER

12

People always say that you're going the wrong way when it's simply a way of your own.
— Angelina Jolie

Angelina Jolie has been a trailblazer in both her career and her personal life. She is living life on her own terms and uses her fame to help bring awareness to many worthy causes. She has shown that being a rebel can inspire a new way of thinking. She takes great risks to advance her career and causes and does not care what other people think when she makes a mistake. Angelina has shown us that being different and going against the crowd can allow us to be ourselves and still be successful. TAKE ACTION: Focus on who you are, what you want, and make it happen. Do it your way.

CHARACTER

13

Stay Hungry. Stay Foolish. — **Steve Jobs**

Steve Jobs is recognized as one of the greatest inventors of our time. His quote is about balance. On the one hand, his work ethic to constantly be creating innovative new products that will impact the world was always at the forefront on his mind.

On the other hand, he recognized that being "foolish" provides that balance we need to allow the creativity to emerge. Steve reminds us that success is achieved when we remain driven and focused on our goals and still take the time to play and have fun. TAKE ACTION: Have balance when chasing your dreams: Work Hard … Have Fun.

CHARACTER

14

Tough times never last, but tough people do.
— **Robert H. Schuller**

Tough times are just part of life. We have all experienced these times to some degree or another. The key is what we make of them. Champions learn from these experiences and apply the lessons to further advance their goals and dreams. We are the champions of our future and know that these tough and challenging times do not last forever. They help us build character and give us the strength to lead ourselves and others to greatness. Never underestimate the heart of a champion. TAKE ACTION: Stay strong no matter the circumstances because hard times do not last forever. Perseverance wins.

CHARACTER

15

The lesson is that you can still make mistakes and be forgiven. — **Robert Downey Jr.**

Mistakes are part of life and something that we have to deal with. Mistakes range from choosing the wrong flavored drink to life-changing mistakes. Life teaches us a lesson regardless of the mistake. The fact is we can be forgiven for the mistake if we are truly sorry. Forgiving ourselves is one of the hardest experiences because we repeatedly remind ourselves of what has happened in the past. Mistakes are also called by other names—experience and wisdom. They can help us avoid making missteps in the future.
TAKE ACTION: Forgive, let go, and find peace within.

CHARACTER

16

The more you know, the less you need to say.
— **Jim Rohn**

As we gain our expertise and confidence, there is no need to brag about what we have done to bring our ideas to fruition. Others will wonder what we are up to by the smile we have on our face all day long. We are working hard to make our dreams and goals come true. The right people are showing up to help us along our success journey. We do not need to say anything because people just know that we are on it. TAKE ACTION: Keep your skills and knowledge up to date. Have an excellent work ethic. Set a world-class example for others.

CHARACTER

17

The world is changed by your example, not by your opinion. —**Paulo Coelho**

We are here to set an example for others. With the noise and confusion in the world, "positive thinking" people do make a difference. We must inspire others who never thought that they, too, could ever succeed. We can show others the way through our examples rather than rendering an opinion of what we think should or could have happened. Everyone on social media has an opinion, but they choose to remain anonymous, mostly. We believe in leading from the front to make our presence known.
TAKE ACTION: Set the kind of example every day that others are inspired to follow.
It is called leadership.

CHARACTER

18

The three great essentials to achieve anything worthwhile are: Hard work, Stick-toitiveness, and Common sense. **– Thomas Edison**

As Entrepreneurs, we naturally have a strong work ethic and use it to achieve our dreams. We move with purpose and conviction toward our goals every day and create the momentum needed to be successful. We create our own opportunities because we believe in making our own good fortune. Our definition of hard work is different from others. We work well into the night and every weekend, knowing that, in the end, our efforts will be rewarded. Studies have shown that, by setting goals and timelines, we can exceed our original conception of success over time.
TAKE ACTION: Keep your work ethic honed to a high standard.

CHARACTER

19

Your critics don't count. They will fade. I won't. — **Justin Timberlake**

It does not matter what our critics say about us. We know that they will always be there no matter what we do or say. Our job is to take what they say and determine if there is anything that we can learn from their perspective. We must let go of the rest of their opinion if it does not help us reach our goals. That is the hardest part: letting go. If we do not, we'll get stuck inside our head and delay our progress. TAKE ACTION: Shake off hurtful words and know that in a short period of time our critics will fade into obscurity, but you will still be going.

CHARACTER

20

Success is how high you bounce when you hit bottom.
— **George S. Patton**

The great part about a new day is that we can create something extraordinary that did not happen yesterday. Every successful billionaire and millionaire has experienced failure in their lives. The difference is that they decided to shake it off, get up and try again until they won. We are millionaires in the making as long as we never give up on our dreams, and, more importantly, on ourselves. We have not come this far to stop and quit forever because we had a setback. TAKE ACTION: Learn from your mistakes and get back in the game as soon as possible with an even greater determination to succeed.

CHARACTER

For continued motivation that will help you develop the character you need to succeed through difficult times, visit **Visionocity_Magazine** on Instagram.

CONFIDENCE

CONFIDENCE

1

A person with a new idea is a crank until the idea succeeds. — **Mark Twain**

Mark Twain had it right. Successful people invent new ways of doing things. They see a solution where others see problems, challenges, and obstacles. This is exactly who we are because we are always looking for a better way. When we succeed, people will talk about how they knew us when we were just getting started with this crazy idea we were always talking about. It is the idea that came to us like a flash of inspiration and we became obsessed with the idea and brought it to life. TAKE ACTION: Follow your passion. Create that life you dream of and deserve.

CONFIDENCE

2

A real friend is one who walks in when the rest of the world walks out. — **Walter Winchell**

We know who our true friends are when we run into hard times. They are the ones who will stand by our side no matter what we have done or said. They are always there to comfort us and give us advice. More importantly, they are there to just listen while we rant endlessly about the situation. A true friend stands by our side to support us through our darkest times with total understanding of who we really are. TAKE ACTION: Show a true friend how grateful you are to have them in your life.

3

Courage is going after Moby Dick in a rowboat and taking the tartar sauce with you. — **Zig Ziglar**

With courage and confidence, we can conquer the world! Confidence is like a well-tailored suit that fits just right no matter the size and the shoes we need to get us to our destination. When we walk with our shoulders back and our head held high, we feel and look like a million bucks. People turn to look at us because they want to know who we are and where we are headed. TAKE ACTION: Step out today in confidence and have the courage to be invincible.

CONFIDENCE

4

Doing is one thing. Doing it right is a whole different story. — **Drake**

Drake reminds us that putting in the extra effort to do things the right way will take us to a whole other level of success. We can do things to just get by and say, "That's good enough," but that attitude will not get us to the level of success we truly want to have. Like great athletes, we must practice the basics over and over again because that is how we learn to do things right. That is how championships are won. TAKE ACTION: No matter where we are today, remember that it is never too late to do the right thing.

CONFIDENCE

5

Great minds discuss ideas. Average minds discuss events. Small minds discuss people.
— **Eleanor Roosevelt**

This quote by Eleanor Roosevelt is as true today as the day these words were spoken. We prefer to exchange ideas on getting ahead because we are focused on our success. We want to make a difference in people's lives and create a community that helps one another. We are not like most people who only want to be accepted by the crowd. Our passion and ideas create a lasting inspiration and impression, which is why we attract smart, positive people. TAKE ACTION: Focus on expanding your ideas through selfeducation and seek others with bright minds to expand on these ideas.

CONFIDENCE

6

If everything seems under control, you're just not going fast enough. — **Mario Andretti**

Being an entrepreneur is about creating momentum, which is messy and sometimes feels like we are out-of-control. Going fast is about experimenting with new ideas. If they work, great; if not, learn from the failure and quickly move forward to the next idea/opportunity. It is through these failures that the greatest inventions have been created, like the Postit™ note, for instance. We never know what we will learn until we try. Progress is never easy nor is it a straight line to the top. Success belongs to those who outlast others who gave up too early because they wanted to micromanage the path to success. TAKE ACTION: Stick to your passion, do not give up, and build some momentum.

CONFIDENCE

7

If you were born poor, it's not your mistake. If you die poor, it is your mistake. — **Bill Gates**

We are meant to succeed regardless of our circumstances. We can create our own destiny as long as we are willing to work hard every day. Our circumstances do not define us because we have the ability to envision a much bigger dream than anyone can imagine. As long as we keep working on our goals, they will come to fruition. We are meant to have an extraordinary life, share it with the people we love, and make a difference in the world by creating a legacy. TAKE ACTION: Stay focused on the goal no matter the circumstances. How your story ends is entirely up to you.

CONFIDENCE

8

I've failed over and over again in my life, and that is why I succeed. — **Michael Jordan**

Michael Jordan knows what it takes to become a champion over and over and over again. He knows what it takes to win and knows that losing is part of the game. Michael says, "I've missed more than 9000 shots. I've lost almost 300 games. 26 times, I've been trusted to take the game-winning shot and missed. I've failed over and over and over again in my life. And that is why I succeed."

Success has a formula, and it means that sometimes we lose more than we win. But never giving up is the key to success. TAKE ACTION: Stay dedicated and focused and success will happen. Failure is just another stepping stone.

CONFIDENCE

9

Success is not final. Failure is not fatal. It's the courage to continue that counts. — **Winston Churchill**

As we continue to work on our dreams and goals, we know there will be some setbacks and failures along the way. These will usher in the next wave of success because we took the time to learn from our failures. But success truly comes from us refusing to give up after a failure. We know that success is just around the corner the next time we get back up from our last setback. Our rewards and successes will come because of our courage to continue no matter what happens. TAKE ACTION: Learn from failure. Stay motivated. Know that it is courage that makes the difference.

CONFIDENCE

10

Tell me and I Forget. Teach me and I Remember. Involve me and I Learn. — **Benjamin Franklin**

We set examples for family and friends when we stay focused and determined to reach our goals. When we make them part of our journey, we are able to involve them and teach them about being successful. Others who become part of our journey are also touched by our actions. The key is that our journey to success is not just about us; it involves people close to us and people who observe us. TAKE ACTION: Create a ripple effect that impacts others on your way to achieving your dreams and goals.

CONFIDENCE

11

The secret to my success is a two-word answer: Know People. — **Harvey S. Firestone**

We need the right people around to help us succeed. They encourage us during the bad times and they celebrate with us during the good times. They are ready to help us reach out to their network of friends when we need just the right skill and talent to carry out our vision. Surrounding ourselves with the right people makes all the difference in the world. We keep our circle of friends tight because we know they have got our back. TAKE ACTION: Increase your network of friends and professional contacts. Always work on expanding your reach.

CONFIDENCE

12

What great thing would you attempt if you knew you could not fail? — **Robert H. Schuller**

Robert H. Schuller poses two interesting questions: What if we could not fail? What would we do? He gets to the core of how to create extraordinary success. It is often our fear of failure that holds us back. By working through our fears at that moment, we summon the courage to get out of our comfort zone and try something new. There is greatness in all of us that's just waiting to come alive once we put aside our fear of failure. TAKE ACTION: Get out of your comfort zone and try something new even if it scares you. Success has a companion called risk.

CONFIDENCE

13

Whatever your dream is go for it.
— **Magic Johnson**

Dreams are nothing more than a bucket list without action behind them. What makes the difference in this world? It is finally deciding to take action. We do not need anyone's permission or approval. Magic Johnson has lived the world of championships along with more than his share of life's setbacks. He has worked to overcome anything that life has thrown his way. He is a champion because he never gave up on his dreams, always believing there was a better tomorrow. TAKE ACTION: Go after your dream no matter what others think and say.

CONFIDENCE

14

You can have anything you want if you are willing to give up the belief that you can't have it.
— **Robert Anthony**

Our greatest obstacle preventing us from achieving success is our belief system that we cannot do something. What we think in our mind and what we believe in our hearts often becomes reality. But once we have the right perspective, we will attract the right people and the right opportunities. We must change our belief system to one that says we can and will achieve anything we set our minds to achieve. We are champions of our destiny. TAKE ACTION: Create a positive attitude that what you want is possible and raise positive outcomes from your belief system.

CONFIDENCE

15

You don't learn to walk by following the rules. You learn by doing and by falling over.
— **Richard Branson**

Sir Richard Branson knows how to build successful businesses. As the billionaire founder of Virgin Atlantic Airline, he has created his own way of doing business. He's always focused on his customers and constantly innovating new company ventures. Equally important, Branson has fun in what he is doing and his organization throughout the world carries on his beliefs and traditions. But it is through correcting his mistakes that he is able to create and leave a lasting legacy for future generations to follow. TAKE ACTION: Experiment with a new idea. Learn from any disappointment and capitalize on it. Success will follow.

CONFIDENCE

16

Your time is limited so don't waste it living someone else's life. — **Steve Jobs**

We are born to be unique and stand above the crowd. It is OK to be different because that is what makes us an original. Like Steve Jobs, we need to embrace who we are no matter what others think or say about us and our ideas. Do not live in someone else's shadow because that is not living. Today is our day to be who we really are. TAKE ACTION: Have the courage to take action on what you really want.

CONFIDENCE

For continued motivation that will give you the confidence you need to believe anything is possible, visit **Visionocity_Magazine** on Instagram.

FOCUS

FOCUS

1

Always do your best. What you plant now you will harvest later. — **Og Mandino**

We should always do our best at whatever we attempt. We must believe that what we do today will have an effect on our future. We may not see the benefits right away but what we plant today will make a difference tomorrow. We may never know how our actions could help others but we know that we must keep moving forward doing our best. For today, we could make that difference in one person's life that could affect them forever. TAKE ACTION: Be your best and do your best today, because your future depends on it.

2

> Think of the long view of life, not just what's going to happen today or tomorrow. Don't give up what you want in life for something you think you want now.
> — **Richard G. Scott**

It easy to rationalize what we want to have today at the expense of our future dreams. Life is about trade-offs and balancing priorities. Success is about discipline and timing, ask any billionaire. This does not mean that we cannot enjoy ourselves along the way. It simply means we need to understand that our dedication to our dream today increases the likelihood of success tomorrow. Life is a series of trade-offs, and we must account for the consequences of our decisions. TAKE ACTION: Ask yourself if you need, or just want, something that will impact your future and understand the distinction between them.

3

Family is the most important thing to me.
— **David Beckham**

Our family is the most important priority we can have. They are far above making money or buying that new car. They are the ones that keep us grounded and help us understand what is truly important in our lives. Our family, and friends who are just like family, will be there to celebrate our victories as well as comfort us when we are tested by life's challenges. David Beckham understands that all the money and celebrity in the world can never take the place of his family. TAKE ACTION: Tell your family and close friends how much they really mean to you.

4

First, they ignore you, then they laugh at you, then they fight you, then you win. — **Mahatma Gandhi**

It seems that, when we have a clear vision in our mind and begin to act on it, people will give us a million reasons why we will fail. They ignore us, and then they make fun of us, and spread rumors about us. When we begin to show some progress in following our dream, they begin to fight us and even hold us back. Throughout this process, we must not pay attention to the naysayers because they have no idea what we are capable of creating. We know in the end we will win. And when we do, we will have the last laugh because we were crazy enough to believe in our dream. TAKE ACTION: Focus on what you want to achieve, have confidence that you can make it happen, then do what it takes to win.

5

Focus on where you want to go not
on what you fear. — **Tony Robbins**

Tony Robbins is one of the greatest motivational coaches ever, and has been a leader in this field for decades. His message has always been to focus on our dreams and desires more than our fears. Every successful person has had to get over their fears to achieve success. There is an acronym that says, "F.E.A.R. is False Evidence Appearing Real." When we create a burning desire for our success over the fear of taking the risk to achieve it that is when we will see massive forward momentum. TAKE ACTION: Get so excited about your dreams that you will want to leave your comfort zone.

6

I never worry about the problem. I worry about the solution. — **Shaquille O'Neal**

Problems can paralyze your thinking by focusing on what is wrong, not what is right. We can become paralyzed when we think there is only one answer to our problem. Such narrowness usually results in increased anxiety and drama in our lives. Instead, we must turn our attention toward the solution and create at least three options. Once we see the different possibilities for how to solve our problem, we regain our confidence that everything will work itself out for the best. TAKE ACTION: Create alternative solutions to your most pressing problems and pick the best option, perhaps what you thought was a mountain turns out to be only a molehill.

7

Insanity: Doing the same thing over and over again and expecting different results. — **Albert Einstein**

Albert Einstein made a brilliant observation with his description of insanity. If we keep trying the same thing over and over again, we are going to keep getting the same old results. Success is achieved by trying something new, failing, learning, and trying again. Yes, it may be painful from time to time, but if we stay in our comfort zone, we will rarely get the exceptional results we are expecting for ourselves. Small steps producing progress every day will create the momentum we need to succeed. TAKE ACTION: Try something new and unusual when working at goals that have seen limited success so far. You may suddenly find something surprising that changes your world.

FOCUS

8

Let's go invent tomorrow rather than worrying about what happened yesterday. **—Steve Jobs**

Steve Jobs has certainly given us so much in the way of firsts in technology and innovation. One of his greatest gifts was his love for the future. His curiosity drove him to create world-changing devices that have impacted the lives of everyone on the entire planet. He was always looking to the future because he believed that whatever happened yesterday should remain there. Each of us has a piece of Steve Jobs' spirit in us. So tomorrow wake up with a renewed commitment to inventing a greater future for ourselves and those we care about. TAKE ACTION: Invent your future and leave yesterday's events behind.

9

> Some people want it to happen; some wish it would happen, others make it happen.
> — **Michael Jordan**

Today is the day to make things happen. We work hard every day and stay committed to never giving up until we win. Others may talk about what they are going to do, and it is the same speech they have given for years. They have vision boards and have read books about positive thinking but never take action on their dreams. They wish for something to happen but nothing ever happens. And nothing will happen until action is taken ... and the hard work begins. We know that it takes perseverance to achieve our goals. TAKE ACTION: Create an action plan and work on it every day until each goal is achieved. Doers succeed.

10

There's no reason to have Plan B because it'll distract your Plan A. — **Will Smith**

When people talk about Plan B, they assume they are going to fail at their Plan A. What a crazy assumption! Will Smith is right. A good Plan A is what we need to stay focused on our goals and dreams. We know that there will be some bumps in the road, but we will never give up on our Plan A. We know that the higher we raise our confidence level and believe in ourselves the closer we will get to the life we have chosen to have. TAKE ACTION: Pick a direction. Create a course of action. Rework the plan until you succeed. Make it count. A Plan B is just an excuse for giving up on Plan A.

11

Today is the only day. Yesterday is gone.
— **John Wooden**

We need to shake off whatever happened yesterday. We cannot change what was said or the events that occurred. If we made a mistake, ask what we have learned from this situation, make peace with it and move on. Today is a fresh start to set things back on the right track. We must never lose sight of the fact that we are here to play the long game and that missteps will happen. TAKE ACTION: Set your intention of making today an extraordinary day.

12

You don't need to be a genius or a college graduate to be successful. You just need a dream. — **Michael Dell**

Many billionaires never finished college but succeeded anyway by building empires. They had a dream, a desire, worked hard and were never willing to give up the fight. They are who they are today because they let nothing stand in their way to becoming successful. You have the same opportunity to be successful as long as you keep showing up every day and working hard toward your dream. TAKE ACTION: Create a dream so big that it is the only thing that you can think about morning, noon, and night.

13

You must be ready not only to take opportunities but to make them. — **Rod Moore**

We know to be on the lookout for new opportunities because we never know when they will come knocking at our door. We need to distinguish between opportunities and a waste of time. The greatest opportunities are the ones we create for ourselves. We are used to thinking differently than the crowd. This is something we get excited about every day because we are consumed with creating our own success. TAKE ACTION: Craft your future through the opportunities that you create for yourself.

FOCUS

For continued motivation that helps you focus on what is important, visit **Visionocity_Magazine** on Instagram.

INSPIRATION

1

Greatness exists in all of us. — **Will Smith**

We are destined for greatness no matter where we are in life at the moment. Will Smith believed in himself and his abilities long before he had any great success. Like Will, our success will arrive in a spectacular manner. We are a work-in-progress, perfecting our craft and gifts. It is often said that others will see the greatness in us, but it is often something that we take for granted. We think, *Everyone can do that. I am not so special.* Believe today that greatness is within you. Keep working and moving forward. Our success is just around the corner! TAKE ACTION: Ask five friends to describe what they admire the most about you.

INSPIRATION

2

I don't design clothes. I design dreams.
— **Ralph Lauren**

We started out to be successful. Part of our journey is to be the answer that others are looking for. The ultimate goal is to create dreams for others like Ralph Lauren has done his entire career. When we help people get what they want, we create a lifetime of success. Entrepreneurs are geared toward creating a business that provides value to their customers. One factor that ties every business together is the desire to make a difference in people's lives regardless of the product or service. TAKE ACTION: Focus on serving others and help them get what they want.

3

I'm thankful to all those who said "No." Because of them, I did it myself. — **Albert Einstein**

As we work on our dream, we hear the word "No" more often than "Yes". We use these rejections to reshape our ideas and approach. It forces us to seek new ways of achieving our goals. "No" is a powerful word because it can discourage us, causing us to abandon our dreams, or it can encourage us to try new ways to have others say, "Yes." TAKE ACTION: Be thankful to those who say, "No," because it makes us look harder for a way to have them say, "Yes," the next time we talk with them.

INSPIRATION

4

It's time to start living the life you have imagined.
— **Henry James**

It is our time to live the life we have long wished to have and be the person we wish to be. Dining at a fine restaurant every night may be on the wish list. Maybe it is having someone take care of the errands that will make life easier on us. Life is about the little things that we do on a daily basis that bring us joy, happiness and a sense of relief from being overwhelmed day in and day out. TAKE ACTION: Start living your life with the imagination of your ideal life.

INSPIRATION

5

Man is still the most extraordinary computer of all.
— **John F. Kennedy**

John Kennedy spoke these words before we had Apple, Google, Facebook, Twitter and those many other advances in technology. These words are as true today as the day Kennedy spoke them. We can imagine and create something from nothing with just an idea. With the changes in technology and crowdfunding, we do not need the traditional bank to start our businesses. We are all entrepreneurs and can make things happen. We use computers to advance our ideas, but the technology is simply a tool to bring our ideas to life. TAKE ACTION: Remember we are more complex and extraordinary than any computer will ever be because we are inspired by our ideas.

INSPIRATION

6

Never give up on what you really want to do. The person with big dreams is more powerful than the one with all the facts. — **H. Jackson Brown, Jr.**

Have you ever noticed that the person who says we cannot succeed is the one who quotes the most facts and statistics? They tell us that the odds of winning are so low that we should give up working those long hours, yet they are the ones still living small and just getting by. What they do not understand is that it is our big dreams that will create our great future regardless of what the numbers and facts say. We are meant to beat the odds. TAKE ACTION: Stay focused and never give up on your dreams and deepest desires.

INSPIRATION

7

No matter what people tell you, words and ideas can change the world. — **Robin Williams**

As Entrepreneurs, we strive to make a difference wherever we can. We work at being excellent at our craft so we can help others while getting closer to our vision and goals. We really believe that one idea can change the world. Knowing this is true, there is every reason to believe that we are the spark to a new way of thinking, and we are working on the next idea that will "go viral". TAKE ACTION: Believe that you can make a difference by standing up for something you believe in.

INSPIRATION

8

Once you make a decision, the universe conspires to make it happen. — **Ralph Waldo Emerson**

When we put our full attention on what we want, the right opportunities and the right people will start to show up. We will begin to see forward movement in ways we have not experienced before. We decide to take action because we are consumed with the idea of our future. Our decision to succeed will start a movement that cannot be stopped until we arrive at our destiny. TAKE ACTION: Believe the universe will conspire for us to win once we decide to show up and work hard for our dreams.

INSPIRATION

9

**One day your life will flash before your eyes.
Make sure it's worth watching.
— From *The Bucket List Movie* - Morgan Freeman**

As dreamers, we dream big dreams. We want a better future for ourselves and our families. What we are creating is so spectacular that we cannot wait to jump out of bed in the morning. We are blessed to have this level of excitement in our lives because our story is one of triumph and victory tempered with moments of challenges, but never defeat. Morgan Freeman read these lines in the movie *The Bucket List* and they are so true.
TAKE ACTION: Create a life that we know is worth watching, because it is, and it is going to be a great ride.

INSPIRATION

10

Start where you are. Use what you have.
Do what you must. **—Arthur Ashe**

Every successful person had a starting point. They started many years ago before they became an *overnight* success. They used their street smarts and determination to drive toward their goal. They did whatever it took to get what they wanted, never gave up and never stopped. These are the exact footsteps we must follow to be successful. We have so many examples and mentors that will give us insights into how and what direction to take so we can be successful. TAKE ACTION: Become a student of successful people and learn how they accomplished their dreams.

INSPIRATION

11

The ones who are crazy enough to think that they can change the world are the ones who do. **— Steve Jobs**

We have an idea that is going to change people's lives for the better. We are told by our friends and family that we are crazy for working those long hours and weekends. Here is the deal: Just because others think we are crazy does not mean that we are going to stop, because we know that we need to be a little crazy to change the world and make a difference. TAKE ACTION: Follow your passion and forget what others say when they try to discourage you.

INSPIRATION

12

We make a living by what we get, but we make a life by what we give. — **Winston Churchill**

We work hard to make a living and move closer to our dreams. By making a difference in other people's lives, we begin to define ourselves in a much broader context. We are not defined by what we acquire throughout our lives but by whom we help along the way. That defines us for who we really are. When we place the needs of others above our needs, we grow in ways that we may not realize at the time. TAKE ACTION: Make a difference in other people's lives as you are building your success. Your riches will grow beyond the money.

13

You pray for rain; you gotta deal with the mud.
— **Denzel Washington**

We wish only the best for ourselves, our friends, and our families. We rejoice when victory comes our way and we see the rewards of our efforts. The reality, though, is that with these moments often come times when we learn life's harder lessons. While we may not like these turns of events, they are part of our journey to success. We are difference-makers, and we will continue to move forward regardless of the circumstances until our goals and dreams are fulfilled.

TAKE ACTION: Recognize that you must celebrate every victory and learn from every setback.

14

You were born to win, but to be a winner, you must plan to win, prepare to win, and expect to win.
— **Zig Ziglar**

Winning is something that requires hard work and dedication, and it takes months and years of pursuing our goals relentlessly. When we hear the words, "overnight sensation," it is rarely true. What observers do not see are the long hours of practice, planning, preparation, and patience that it took to get there. In addition, it is your *expectation* that winning is inevitable that creates the possibility of winning in the first place. TAKE ACTION: See it in your mind first and create what you want for yourself.

INSPIRATION

For continued motivation that will help you create the opportunities that will provide life-long success, visit **Visionocity_Magazine** on Instagram.

STRENGTH

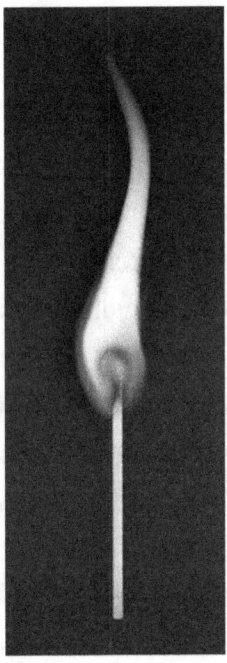

1

A person who never made a mistake never tried anything new. — **Albert Einstein**

Success comes from trying something new, failing and trying it again. Most people will readily offer their opinion about what we should and should not do but they will ultimately stay in their comfort zone and risk nothing new themselves. They want others to stay the course with them and have their world remain constant all the while offering their opinion on how things should be done. We need to surround ourselves with people who have a sense of adventure, people who expand our world and create a better life for us and our families. TAKE ACTION: Learn something new today and see what happens tomorrow.

STRENGTH

2

Don't give up on your dream or your dream will give up on you. **—John Wooden**

We need to stay dedicated to our dreams and chase them every day. If not, we will lose interest and will defeat ourselves before we even begin. No one else will come to our rescue unless we believe in ourselves. What creates abundance is the pursuit of a dream. It is what keeps us going after it, day and night, to the point of obsession.
TAKE ACTION: Don't ever give up on your dream because you deserve everything life has to give you.

3

Haters are the people who will broadcast your failures and whisper your success. — **Will Smith**

Some people are always ready to talk behind our backs, spreading rumors that are not true. These haters are always ready to put us down. What they do not understand is that we refuse to listen to any of their negativity. We continue to do what we do best: work on our success. And when we do succeed, they are the last ones to utter any praise. That is why they will remain small and silent while we will achieve our big dreams. TAKE ACTION: Stay focused on your goals and dreams. Haters are just part of the journey. Ignore them.

STRENGTH

4

I don't have to be what you want me to be.
I'm free to be what I want. — **Muhammad Ali**

We do not have to listen to what others think we should be, do or say. We have very specific goals in mind, and we have a plan for how to get them. Our critics can follow us or get out of our way. We know what we want, and we will work every day until we get it. We're here to set an example for the doubters who said, "It cannot be done."
TAKE ACTION: Give yourself permission
to stand above the crowd and become
who you are destined to be.

STRENGTH

5

If you don't build your dreams, someone will hire you to build theirs. — Tony Gaskin

We want our dreams to come true so badly that we think about them all the time. But if we only "think" about our dreams, they will forever remain on our wish list or our bucket list and never become reality. We will remain in a job, working long hours for someone else, and complaining that, "It is just not right the way they're doing things." With a shift in our attitude and mindset, we can fulfill our own dreams. TAKE ACTION: Build your dream. Start small. Start today. And never give up!

STRENGTH

6

Laugh as much as you can. Breathe and love as long as you live. — **Johnny Depp**

Laughter is one of the best medicines we can take. It helps us in so many ways. It lifts our spirits and rejuvenates us in an instant. With all the pressures around us, we need to have a relief outlet from our constant focus on our goals. Johnny Depp's quote anchors us to what's truly important in life. Our sense of humor helps us get through the day when things get crazy. TAKE ACTION: Find something to laugh at today.

STRENGTH

7

Never allow someone to be your priority while allowing yourself to be their option.
— **Mark Twain**.

Sometimes we get blinded by other people's friendship. We want to be part of their lives and mingle with their group of friends so much that we are willing to have our interests take a back seat.

But often we find they do not keep their commitments to us and then we *make excuses* for their bad behavior. We must never place ourselves in second place. We must surround ourselves with supportive and like-minded people. TAKE ACTION: Respect yourself enough to be your own priority.

STRENGTH

8

Never. Never. Never give up. — **Winston Churchill**

Winston Churchill is famously known for saying, "Never. Never. Never give up." He knew the importance of perseverance until the end goal is accomplished. History is full of examples where, in spite of the defeats, victory was achieved in the long run by refusing to quit. We have great mentors, who have shown us how to overcome challenges, problems, and obstacles that are standing in our way. We will overcome and be successful because we refuse to give up under any circumstances. No one will deny us victory.
TAKE ACTION: Find a mentor that will help you through the tough times and never give up.

STRENGTH

9

Sometimes life hits you in the head with a brick. Don't lose faith. — **Steve Jobs**

Today may have been a rough day. Things did not work out as we had planned or expected. People did not keep their promises. They did not show up for the appointment or unkind words were exchanged. It was a lousy day today. Take it all in stride. Shake it off because, if you don't, the naysayers win. We will not let that happen. As Steve Jobs said, "Keep the faith." Tomorrow, we get to start again, and things will work out as we planned. TAKE ACTION: Ask, "What can I learn from this setback I have experienced?" Then set about making it right.

STRENGTH

10

The best investment you can make is in yourself.
— **Warren Buffet**

Our education is just beginning the day after we leave school. That is when we start learning from the masters of success such as Warren Buffet. Through their actions and writings, these billionaires and millionaires tell us what they did to succeed, including their greatest failures. They show us how they overcame obstacles and adversity and found answers to many other problems. We can learn from them. TAKE ACTION: Continue to invest in yourself until you succeed just like the titans of business did.

STRENGTH

11

When you drive yourself further once the effort gets painful, you will win. — **Roger Bannister**

Winners know how to accept the fact that challenges are simply part of the journey. As winners, we will not quit at the first sign of trouble. On the contrary, we know how to learn from these situations and use them to our advantage in the future. That is the difference between winners and losers. We do not mind a little disappointment every once in a while. It keeps us at the top of our game. Roger Bannister was the first man to run a mile in less than 4 minutes. TAKE ACTION: Learn to push past the disappointments and painful lessons to obtain the success you seek.

STRENGTH

12

Life is what happens to you while you're busy making other plans. **—John Lennon**

We make plans that do not always work out. It is called "Life is happening". We have experienced the stress of things not working out the way we thought they would. We cannot stop because of these circumstances. It is just life, and we will not let it stop us from achieving our dreams. We have the tenacity to continue hustling regardless of any setback because absolutely no one or nothing will stop us. TAKE ACTION: Learn to accept that life does not always work out the way you planned and make the best of any situation you are handed.

STRENGTH

For continued motivation that will help you find the strength to overcome everyday challenges, visit **Visionocity_Magazine** on Instagram.

ONE FINAL THOUGHT

With everything buzzing around us moving so quickly and with great disruption, each of us needs some encouragement that our future still holds the hope and promise of a better life. We seek inspiration and motivation through every type of social media to keep our hopes and dreams alive. We might sign up for a daily motivational message to be delivered to our mobile device or we spend time reading books and blogs, listening to podcasts, or looking at videos that will keep that spark alive telling us that anything is possible. A simple message of encouragement that we read can stay in our mind all day, making it easy to recall in those moments when things may not be going so well.

Businesses have even turned to the power of storytelling to create a greater connection with their audience. Sharing an emotional moment that tells their customers, "I understand how you feel," is one of the most powerful ways to connect with their customers. We want to feel like we're connected to a broader community of like-minded people. It's through this connection that we find our mental reinforcement and feel we belong to something much bigger than ourselves.

Ignite Your Inspiration and become a difference-maker in people's lives. Be motivated to share your unique gifts and talents that will impact at least one person who needed to hear your message. Be bold in dreaming big dreams. Be determined and believe in yourself. Believe that one day your dreams will become reality.

ABOUT THE AUTHOR

Lucy Hoger is a successful Board Member, CEO and Senior Executive with a track record for propelling organizations and companies to the next level of profitable achievement within their highly competitive markets. She has proven herself repeatedly as a leader in spearheading the turnaround of potential business failures into business successes. She possesses an exceptional ability to develop and retain leadership teams selected from the "best of the best" talent that creates results-driven technology and business innovation.

Her unique expertise was honed by her background as a strategic consultant with Price Waterhouse and Gemini Consulting. That experience, combined with her career-long real-world performance for several NASDAQ companies, brings a unique insight into problem-solving for any business situation. She has served on the Board of Directors for twelve companies providing business growth guidance.

ABOUT THE AUTHOR

She publishes an internationally ranked digital magazine, *Visionocity*, which is focused on providing practical advice from contributing business owners who are succeeding in today's challenging environment. She also is a source of motivation and inspiration to over a hundred thousand followers worldwide through her Instagram account. She's gained insights into strategic trends that position her clients for exponential business advancement.

As an accomplished speaker, Lucy has spoken at Rice University for their MBA Program on Leadership. The speech was entitled: The Answer to the Upcoming Labor Crisis. She's also been the keynote speaker for Women in Primerica, one of the nation's leading financial services firms. She's been interviewed by a leading syndicated Chicago radio station to provide business advice to their listening audience.

She also provides strategic positioning for businesses that wish to create and promote new products and services, and conducts leadership workshops for individuals to help them expand their careers and businesses.

www.ingramcontent.com/pod-product-compliance
Lightning Source LLC
Chambersburg PA
CBHW070253190526
45169CB00001B/396